VOICE TRAINING
FOR
CHOIRS AND SCHOOLS

VOICE TRAINING

FOR

CHOIRS AND SCHOOLS

by

CYRIL BRADLEY ROOTHAM, M.A., Mus.D.

Organist and Choirmaster,
St John's College, Cambridge

Cambridge:
at the University Press
1912

CAMBRIDGE
UNIVERSITY PRESS

University Printing House, Cambridge CB2 8BS, United Kingdom

Cambridge University Press is part of the University of Cambridge.

It furthers the University's mission by disseminating knowledge in the pursuit of education, learning and research at the highest international levels of excellence.

www.cambridge.org
Information on this title: www.cambridge.org/9781107504943

© Cambridge University Press 1912

First published 1912
First paperback edition 2015

A catalogue record for this publication is available from the British Library

ISBN 978-1-107-50494-3 Paperback

PREFACE

THIS little work is an amplification of a paper on Choir-Boy Training read by invitation before the International Congress of Musicians in London (May, 1911). Since that occasion I have received from several different quarters requests that my paper should appear in book form. After I had decided to respond to these expressions of good-will, it was suggested to me that the project might be extended to meet the requirements of singing-classes in schools, whether of boys or girls. Hence the present form and scope of the work.

The subject is one of great importance, and presents many hard problems. No one is more conscious than I that boys' and girls' voices cannot be trained successfully by mere book-reading. Only practical experience can solve the difficulties which beset the teacher. The task I have attempted is to indicate to those who have little or no experience the directions in which lie both those difficulties and their probable solution.

I wish to acknowledge my obligation to many who have written before me on different branches of the subject. But most of all am I indebted to my father, Daniel Wilberforce Rootham, whose early training taught me to think on these matters, whose profound knowledge of the human voice has been my constant guide—to whom finally I am indebted for several useful suggestions during his reading of my proof-sheets.

C. B. R.

CAMBRIDGE,
October, 1912.

CONTENTS

CONTENTS

EXERCISES

CHAPTER I

INTRODUCTORY

VALUE OF VOCAL TRAINING FOR BOYS AND GIRLS

No one will question the potential charm of young voices, whether 'Natural singing. of boys or of girls. It is necessary to use the qualifying word 'potential,' for many unthinking people still believe that the voices of children (i.e. the voices of those who have not reached the age of puberty) sound best in their 'natural' state. Let us examine the word 'natural' in this connection. If the use of this term be meant to convey the spontaneous and perhaps unconscious outburst of song from a healthy and happy child, of course it would be idle to dispute the charm of the young voice. But when does nature end and art begin? Bad habits are as easily acquired in singing as in any other department of life. The voice of the newspaper-boy in our streets is 'natural' enough; for surely no classes exist to train boys' voices for calling the titles and contents of newspapers. Similarly, children at their games use their voices 'naturally'; but all voice-trainers know the damage that frequently results to both the speaking voices and the singing voices of children who are allowed to shout constantly and without restraint. The truth is that singing is an art, even for children, who may, and Singing an art. should, be carefully taught to speak and sing properly from quite an early age. If the teachers be competent, there need be no fear of any taint of artificiality; for the 'art that conceals art' is a lesson that can and must be learnt as soon as possible.

Singing a healthy exercise.

Singing is a healthy exercise in itself. The full expansion of the lungs necessary for intelligent singing (however youthful the performer) is beneficial from the physical point of view. In schools it is valuable especially as an outlet for pent-up nervous energy. Healthy boys and girls, who are obliged to sit more or less in one position, often without speaking, for an hour at a time in a class-room, will welcome the interpolation of a singing hour: and the masters or mistresses who have charge of the same pupils before or after the singing hour will welcome it equally.

Singing an education.

Singing is also an education and a relaxation of the mind. It is essentially different from other forms of study, and is therefore a stimulating contrast to ordinary class-work. Further, from the purely musical point of view, singing at sight is an admirable way of training the eye and ear to understand time and rhythm, intervals, phrasing and expression. Thus it provides a firm foundation for the grasp of the more intricate forms of instrumental music, whether the young singers in later years are to become performers or intelligent listeners.

CHAPTER II

TREATMENT OF THE YOUNG VOICE

Boys' and girls' voices more or less the same.

APPARENTLY no material difference exists between the normal voices of boys and of girls. Broadly speaking, the voices of girls of any given age are likely to be less resonant and more restricted in compass than those of boys of the same age: but it is an open question whether the modern girl, with her increased facilities for exercise and outdoor games, will not soon make good this deficiency. However that may be, it seems certain that the same methods of training will suit both girls and boys equally well up to the age of puberty. Of course children of nine years of age will not have the same physique as those who are fourteen. The lungs of the younger children will not usually be able to sustain high notes or long phrases as well as those of their elders—a consideration that should always be borne in mind by teachers. This fact, however, should not prevent the exercise of even the youngest voices. Boys and girls may begin to sing as soon as they shew any desire to do so. In any case they may start at the age of eight years, provided always that they are not allowed either to shout (i.e. force their voices) or to sing too long at a time. These points will be discussed more fully in chapters IV and V. In considering the question of the wider compass of the boy's voice, especially in the upper notes, it must be remembered that the same range does not appear in all boys, nor in all girls, alike. It is very doubtful, nevertheless, whether girls before the age of puberty should ever sing a real contralto part; similarly it is extremely rare to find a true alto voice in a boy[1].

The few selected boys belonging to a cathedral or good church choir will possess voices with an extensive compass, and will have the advantages of regular and constant training: whereas the larger school class or chorus will of necessity include boys' or girls' voices of varying compass, and lacking the same opportunities of regular supervision and instruction. The latter, therefore, should not usually be called upon to sing music of so wide a range or of so exacting a nature as the former. *Difference between cathedral choirs and school choruses.*

Singing classes of boys or of girls should occasionally, if possible, hear each other sing. Each might learn something from the other. The boys might gain delicacy, and the girls breadth of tone.

[1] See chapter X, page xli.

CHAPTER III

THE TEACHER[1] AND HIS QUALIFICATIONS

Responsibility of training young voices. ALL who undertake the responsibility of training children's voices should feel quite certain of their fitness for so important a task. Primarily, they should recognise that they have it in their power to make or mar a certain number of the voices of the *next* generation of men or women. Not only the singing voice, but the speaking voice is equally at stake: for it seems at least probable that bad training, or want of training, is responsible for many of the unmusical voices that we hear every day. The possession of a beautiful speaking voice is of distinct value to practically every civilised human being. School teachers and choirmasters seem hardly to realise to what extent they can be directly and indirectly responsible in this respect for the present, and therefore the future, success of the children placed under them. It is surely then of great importance that the teacher should possess **Singing powers of the teacher.** a pleasant and expressive speaking voice, and that he should be able himself to sing, musically and efficiently. He need not be a highly-trained soloist, but he should understand the principles of voice-production and elocution, and should be able to illustrate his lessons for his choir in a practical manner. Children are essentially imitative, and are quick to learn the faults as well as the virtues of their teachers. **Organists as choirmasters.** An organist, in particular, should not be choirmaster unless his vocal experience be at least as thorough as his knowledge of the organ: for the human voice is far more delicate and more expressive than a pipe-organ.

Enthusiasm. Further, the teacher must possess enthusiasm for his work, and sympathy with the needs of his pupils. Most boys and girls have

[1] The term 'teacher,' throughout, is intended to include choirmasters, school-masters and schoolmistresses. The context will decide for whom the remarks are suitable.

imagination and enthusiasm, which merely need the corresponding qualities in the teacher to be magnetized into a powerful force. Nothing is more depressing than a listless and perfunctory singing-lesson or choir-practice: for singing above all things must be a real pleasure to all concerned—an expansion of bodily and mental energies. The thoughts and words of the teacher may be admirable as regards their matter, but if they are to influence the minds of the pupils, they need to be quickened by a genial manner and obvious enthusiasm at the moment.

In a church choir, where the boys are few and of varying ages, the *youngest* should understand all that is going on: for as the older boys leave, the juniors become the seniors, and should have acquired beforehand all the requisite knowledge for their more responsible position. The choirmaster must also take the trouble to know each of his boys and their qualifications. By watching the individual performance of each boy from day to day (not a difficult matter for a man whose heart is in his work), he can notice which boys are improving, which are remaining stationary or are deteriorating: the latter should be admonished or encouraged as the occasion demands, with unfailing regularity. The value of encouragement, especially to sensitive children, is often overlooked.

Choristers as individuals.

CHAPTER IV

FORMATION OF A CHURCH CHOIR OR SCHOOL CHORUS

THE requirements of a school chorus differ from those of a church choir in so many details (notably in numbers, and therefore in the standard of musical efficiency), that it will be convenient to discuss them separately. We will begin with the organisation of a church choir.

A. *Formation of a Church Choir*

The treble part in a church choir is almost invariably sung by boys, whose voices, more colourless and less emotional than those of women, are eminently suitable for the rendering of good music written for the church service.

Choir schools. Most of our cathedrals and collegiate chapels and many of our most important churches possess special choir schools. These schools, of course, provide for the general education of their scholars, though the boys whom they educate are chosen in the first instance for the excellence of their voices and their musical ability. The majority of such boys benefit in various ways during their later life from the vocal and general musical training which they have thus received. A certain number become solo singers, organists and choirmasters, or composers. Thus a good tradition ought to be handed on from generation to generation.

It must not be forgotten that the majority of the choristers who are thus trained come from what we call our lower middle classes. Some people maintain that the best results can be achieved only with boys of so-called gentle birth. It is difficult to believe that this is really the case. Good results are attained only by sympathetic training on sound lines: also good voices and musical intelligence are to a large extent gifts of nature which know nothing of class distinctions. A famous choir school, it is true, can select the best boys from all parts of the country, just as a rich football club can command the services of the best professional players to represent a certain county or district.

Provincial and country churches. But there are many choirmasters who produce good results from purely local material: they have at any rate the satisfaction of knowing that they are really helping the musical needs of their neighbourhood. Of course a village produces fewer boys than a large town : but the village church is the cathedral of its district, and should be recognised as such.

Year by year the village schools are being provided with more competent teachers, who are learning from the highest educational sources that the singing hour is at least as important as any other hour of study. Only let this ideal be followed up by the church and civil authorities of the district, and the choirmaster will have no difficulty in securing time during the week to make his choristers efficient singers for the Sunday services.

Under such circumstances there should be vocal material enough for an efficient choirmaster in practically every church in the country. He should be able to procure, say, fourteen trebles able to sing a simple service well. For the more ornate cathedral service a larger selection of voices and more training will be required.

As regards the question of demand and supply in the matter of boys' voices, it must not be supposed that all boys have musical voices. **Can all boys sing?** A singing-teacher of considerable notoriety has said that *everybody* should be able to sing, and has cited the analogy of birds to support his contention. But can all birds sing? Do even the so-called 'singing' birds all possess equally good voices? Surely some of us at least have heard thrushes and blackbirds singing badly, or busily practising. So some boys have poor voices: others cannot sing at all. Nevertheless, let us but give more time and trouble to the care of children's voices, and a correspondingly larger number of good singers will surely be the result.

In forming or recruiting a church choir, it is well to choose quite young boys of eight or nine, sometimes ten years of age, before they **Forming or recruiting a church choir.** have had many opportunities of acquiring bad vocal habits. At the same time it is advisable to have the choristers, collectively, as much as possible of varying ages, so as to minimize the risk of losing several boys of about the same age at one time, in consequence of the 'breaking' of their voices (i.e. the change of the treble to the adult voice). In choosing a boy for a choir, the voice of course must be

Tests.

thought of first. But other considerations are important. Does he seem intelligent? Can he instantly and accurately reproduce notes of varying pitch and tonality (e.g.) as they are sounded one by one on a pianoforte? These two points should receive careful attention: for even a beautiful voice is of little use, unless the owner have a quick ear and an intelligent brain, even at the age of eight or nine.

Types of voices.

The choirmaster should refuse boys who, in talking or singing, shew traces of harshness or hoarseness, which obviously are not caused by a temporary cold. The voices which will most repay his training are those (not necessarily of great volume) which are clear and even throughout this compass: . Those which betray a bad 'break' about should be avoided: also those which are strong in the lower register and weak in the upper. Further, it is well to find out at once (not a difficult matter, after a little experience) if there be any indication of enlarged tonsils or adenoid growths. These common defects, which can be cured by a simple surgical operation, may be detected usually by the presence of a certain thickness of speech or of somewhat stertorous breathing and an habitually open mouth.

The treble part of the choir, when formed, should consist of 14 or 16 boys, varying in age from about 9 to 15 or 16.

B. *Formation of a School Chorus*

School Chorus.

A school chorus will consist usually of all those pupils who wish to sing. They may be divided into classes, according to age, or they may be massed into one large chorus, and drilled in a body. In either

case one initial test should be enforced. Every boy or girl should be Tests.
required first to sing notes of varying pitch (see previous section on
choirs) when sounded on a pianoforte, one note at a time. Unless these
candidates be able to produce at any given moment the exact pitch
of the note required, they should not be admitted into the singing-class
or chorus, at any rate at first. On the other hand they should not of
necessity be banished from the singing-practice. If they are anxious
to be present, they should be ranged together near the performers, and
have copies of the music. They may possibly improve their musical
sense by listening to the others, and thus in time qualify for the chorus:
in any case they will gain instruction and enjoyment, and will often
prove excellent critics of the work which is being done.

CHAPTER V

PROCEDURE IN THE PRACTICE-ROOM

THE same arrangement will be adopted here as in the preceding
chapter. Procedure in the practice-room will be discussed under two
headings, (A) for church choirs, (B) for schools.

A. *Church Choirs*

In the practice-room, the boys should not actually sing for more Length of
practice.
than about 40 minutes at any one period. If the time allowed for
rehearsal be an hour, there should be short intervals of rest, during
which the theoretical side of the music may be discussed. But, above
all, the boys should not be compelled to stand or sit for too long at Standing or
sitting
a time: if so, they will get cramped and restless, and careless singing position.
will be the result. While they are actually singing, the boys should
stand, or sit on high stools, but with their feet on the ground, in an
easy and natural position: and no part of their bodies should at any

time be in a tense or rigid condition. As in violin or pianoforte playing, for instance, ease of posture should be an essential feature.

Instrument for accompaniment. A pianoforte, and not a harmonium, should be used in the practice-room for accompanying purposes. The pianoforte should be preferably either of the 'grand,' or of the miniature 'cottage' type, so that the choirmaster may see his boys easily. A harmonium is at any time a dismal and pernicious instrument, and it is certainly a bad medium for the accompaniment of boys' or girls' voices. Its nasal tone may be imitated by those who have to sing to it, and it has not the means of 'percussion'—so necessary to mark the varying rhythms of the music to be sung—which are possessed by a pianoforte or a modern organ.

Arrangement and positions of the choristers. The boys should be grouped, Decani to the right, Cantoris to the left of the pianoforte, converging so as to form a rough semicircle away from the instrument. As to the individual positions of the different boys, the usual plan, both at practice and at service-time, is to place the senior boy on each side of the choir at one end of the line, the next senior boy by his side, and so on, the youngest and least trained boy being farthest from the eldest and most experienced. The point of this procedure, no doubt, is that in service-time the head boys shall be nearest the congregation, and so be heard best. A different plan will now be suggested. Let us suppose that there are 14 choristers. At service-time the senior boy on each side of the choir will be placed *in the middle*: on either side of him will be the two youngest boys, of least experience: at each end of the line we shall have those who are second and third in seniority, and next to them will be the two remaining boys of intermediate age and experience. Thus the younger boys will have one more highly trained on either their right or their left: and, as small boys are imitative, the choirmaster can attain in this way both efficiency and a good tradition of singing more easily than by the other method, which produces the maximum of efficiency at one end of the line and the minimum at the other.

In addition to the regular choristers, there should be practising- **Probationers.** boys or probationers, about six in number. These should attend all rehearsals, and should then be placed next to the most experienced choristers. They will form a reserve force, and can be drafted one by one into the choir as vacancies occur. In this way the choirmaster will never have any quite inexperienced boys in his choir at service-time.

It is well to have a regular system of promotion among the **Senior and junior boys.** choristers. The promotion should depend on merit, not necessarily **Promotion.** on seniority, though the one will usually imply the other. With a choir of 14 boys, it is suggested that the three oldest boys on each side should be called 'seniors,' and the other four 'juniors.' The juniors should often be asked to sing by themselves, with or without the pro- bationers, who in turn should sing occasionally without the regular choristers. All choristers, senior and junior, should be required to sing **Solo-singing.** short solos or verse-parts by themselves. Every boy thus accustoms himself, as early as possible, to the sound of his own voice, unsupported by others, and so gradually gains confidence. In this way, too, the questionable system of having only one, or at the most two boys, to sing all the solo passages, is obviated.

Regularity of training, especially in the matter of technical exercises, **Regularity of training.** is of great importance. If the music to be practised in any one week **Exercises.** should take more time than the choirmaster suspected, it would be well to leave the service or anthem, in a measure, to take care of itself, and not to encroach on the valuable 10 minutes or more of vocal exercises, which should be the chief feature of every practice[1]. (This advice is given on the assumption that most of the boys have been trained to read well at sight: for without such training, no musical service can be rendered adequately.)

All the boys should 'beat time' (from their wrists) during the **Beating time.**

---

[1] See chapter XI.

practice of every piece of music. This custom is of the greatest importance in teaching children time-values and rhythm[1].

Singing by sight rather than by ear. However simple the music to be performed, the choristers should never be encouraged or even allowed to sing by ear. From the beginning all probationers must be taught to read at sight, so that after 12 months' training (or earlier) even the youngest boy will have learnt to read fairly difficult music with comparative ease. **Tonic sol-fa system.** The tonic sol-fa system is recommended for a start, provided that it soon be followed by the staff notation, which will, of course, be the medium used for all practical purposes of singing and playing. The employment of the tonic sol-fa system, however, in the earliest stages, will be found a sure means of establishing both diatonic and chromatic intervals in any key firmly in the mind of the least clever boy. Every choirmaster will find that a difficult melodic passage will be at once simplified by translating the notes into the language of the tonic sol-fa system.

The use of the blackboard for purposes of illustrating difficulties is recommended.

Ear-tests. The choristers' sense of pitch should be tested regularly. Some boys will have natural gifts in this direction: others, with practice, can acquire some proficiency in this important branch of musical training. The choirmaster should begin by sounding a note on the pianoforte. He should then find out whether any boy can give the name of the note sounded. If no one be able to do this, he should then tell the boys the name of the note, and try them with an easier problem, by sounding a perfect 5th or major 3rd above the keynote already sounded. Usually some boys will be found who can answer correctly, especially after a little practice. He can then proceed to strike chromatic intervals, or two notes together, or even a chord of three or four notes, asking the

---

[1] The only exception to this rule should be when modal music of the 16th and 17th centuries is being sung. The bar-lines in such cases are modern additions merely to help the eye (see chapter VII, p. xxxii).

boys to tell him first how many notes have been sounded, and then the names of the notes. After that he can play some bars of music in a certain key, and ask the boys to name the key. With experience some of the choir will be found capable of telling him when he modulates, and the names of the keys through which the modulations have occurred. He should be sure that all the boys know the different effects of the major and minor common chords and of the major and minor scales, including both the harmonic and melodic forms of the latter. Further, if (as is to be hoped), the choristers have to sing music written by composers of the 16th and early 17th centuries, they should be taught the elements at any rate of modal composition[1]. The Decani and Cantoris sides of the choir should good-humouredly be pitted against each other, both in answering questions and in actual singing. Each side may occasionally be asked to criticise the performance of the other. *(Major and minor keys. Modes.)*

Every piece of music performed should as far as possible be roughly analysed. The key-signatures and time-signatures must be known: difficult modulations should be pointed out and thoroughly understood. The choirmaster should be sure that all the choristers have grasped his explanations, by the simple expedient of asking some of them, especially the younger boys, to repeat in their own words what they have just heard. *(Analysis of music performed.)*

It will be found that, though physically and mentally the boys themselves will be fresh and alert in the earlier morning hours, their voices will usually not be as clear and manageable as in the afternoon or evening. For this reason it will be well to collect the choristers in the practice-room for about 10 minutes before the Sunday morning service, and 'loosen' their voices by some simple scales and exercises. On such occasions soft singing is best. The small amount of extra trouble taken by the choirmaster in this and other respects already mentioned, will be well repaid by the results. *(Vocal practice before service.)*

[1] See chapter VII, page xxxii.

B. *Schools.*

It is suggested that the school-teacher should read the foregoing section (A) in this chapter, as much of the matter contained in it will be found to be applicable to schools, if the difference in the number of pupils and the amount of time allowed for singing-practice be borne in mind. The paragraphs especially on Length of practice, Standing or sitting position, Instrument for accompaniment, Beating time, Singing by sight rather than by ear, and Analysis of music performed, may be read by school-teachers.

As regards the number of hours allowed for singing-practice during the week, the master or mistress will no doubt be dependent on the school time-table and on the will of the headmaster or headmistress. Assuming, however, that any one practice will not last more than an hour, the time spent in actual singing will vary with the ages of the pupils. Infants, of course, cannot sing for as long a time at a stretch as older boys and girls. Very slight experience will enable the teachers to know when they should stop singing. The little voices will tire and will sing flat, and eagerness will give way to obvious weariness. In the cases of older boys and girls the suggestions in section (A) on 'length of practice,' may be followed.

CHAPTER VI

PRODUCTION OF TONE

Breathing.   Every choirmaster and school-teacher should make it clear to his or her pupils that good singing is impossible without a copious and well-managed supply of breath. The most beautiful organ-pipe or orchestral wind-instrument sounds feeble or grotesque if the wind-supply that makes it speak be insufficient or fitful. Similarly the human voice, by far the most expressive melodic instrument in existence, depends primarily on the supply of breath from the lungs for sustaining tone, for expression and for phrasing. Proper breathing for the purposes of singing and public speaking must be taught; since for the ordinary business of life—whether we sit still, or walk, or talk with others—it is usually not necessary either to expand the lungs to anything like their full capacity, or to breathe with regulated steadiness. But without these two last conditions, good singing is impossible. Once more, singing is an art, even for quite young people. In schools where physical culture has its appointed and regular place, the work of the singing teacher will be lightened; for systems such as Swedish Drill insist on good breathing from the beginning. The pupil will be taught to take in breath through the nose rather than the mouth—a useful accomplishment for anyone who lives in an English town, where fogs and a smoke-laden atmosphere are prevalent : for the nasal passages act as a filter, whereas the mouth obviously does not. Further, by learning to take in breath through the nose, singers will learn at an early age the importance of being able to avoid taking in draughts of cold or damp air through the mouth, especially on coming out of a warm indoor atmosphere at night into the streets. Nevertheless, in spite of the obvious advantages of being able to take breath through the nasal passages only, it is doubtful whether boys and girls should always follow this plan during their singing-practice. Slow and sustained breathing is of great importance; but often the singer has to take a quick and yet a deep breath. In the latter case, if the breath be taken quickly through the nose alone, an audible 'sniff' must result; if through the mouth only, a 'gasp' will be heard. It seems but reasonable in such cases to employ all the means given us by nature, and to breathe through the nose and mouth at the same moment, so that the lungs can be filled quickly and noiselessly. Breathing through the nose alone, then, must be acknowledged a useful and even a necessary accomplishment for boys and girls: but when this desirable habit has been acquired, it seems reasonable that during the actual singing-practice, they should be encouraged to take breath through the nose and the mouth at the same time. The breath should be taken into the lungs without any visible effort, such as raising the shoulders or stiffening the body.

The 'break.' Upper and lower registers. In most boys' and girls' voices (in those of boys especially) a 'break'

or division is likely to appear, usually about . This break

may be accentuated by lack of training or by bad methods of singing. We will call that part of the voice which lies below this division the lower register, and the higher notes beyond it the upper register. To blend these two parts of the voice into one even compass, so that no division can be detected, is perhaps the most difficult part of the choirmaster's work. Unfortunately, through lack of time and opportunity, the school-teacher frequently cannot properly attend to this important problem: so that in a large school class or chorus, some of the pupils' voices (especially those of boys) become harsh and uneven. The danger is that the lower part of the voice will become stronger, while the upper notes—the more beautiful part of at any rate the boy's voice—will then become weak, or perhaps will disappear altogether. An allusion was made in chapter I to an extreme example of this fault—the case of the boy who sells newspapers in the street. His lower register is magnificently strident, but his upper register is non-existent from the singing point of view—the result of constant shouting. To obviate **Different methods of training.** the danger of forcing the lower notes, choirmasters resort to various devices. Some, it is true, try to develop the lower as well as the upper part of the voice to the full. This method is hazardous. There is always the danger of the break appearing, and the lower notes generally become somewhat coarse. The effect may be palliated if we listen to the voices at a distance in a large and resonant building; but at close quarters the tone is unpleasant. Other choir trainers cut the Gordian knot and never allow the voices to develop a full and resonant tone in any part of their compass. This method shuns the difficulty. It follows that there is no 'ring' in the voices, even on the highest notes. Others again, realising that on certain vowel sounds the lower notes cannot be forced, use these 'closed' sounds for all vocal exercises. Others go even further. When actual words are being sung, these closed sounds are being substituted at all times for those particular vowels which might induce the lower register to be too prominent. This method usually makes nonsense of the words, and produces permanently a 'smothered' effect, which, to the listener, is unnatural and irritating. Boys' and girls' voices are really effective only when the words are plainly heard. Vowels as well as consonants must be both clear and natural.

The best way out of the difficulty seems to lie in a compromise. A wise composer, if he be setting words to be sung by a tenor or baritone voice, does not write much for the lowest notes of the singer's compass, since that part of the voice is usually somewhat dull and lacking in power. Similarly, the lower register of the boy's voice (if not of the average girl's) should not be expected to produce the same full and resonant effect as the upper, if the voice be well trained. The upper

notes, above , should be fully developed, and should be carried

downwards into the lower register: the lower register should not be forced upwards to meet the higher. For this reason the exercises at the end of the book will be found to begin mostly on the upper notes. By such means boys' voices especially will be less likely to develop a break, than if they were constantly to be singing exercises which began in the lower register. Also, the higher notes will thus

Exercises beginning on the high notes.

usually be attacked with more certainty when sung away from the practice-room. The pupils should early be taught to concentrate their minds on producing the tone *forward*, just behind the front teeth, so that the small resonance-cavities in the front of the head should be brought fully into requisition to reinforce the voice. Girls, and par-

Vocalising on 'ah' and 'ŏŏ.' ticularly boys, should vocalise on the sound 'ah' in the upper register, and relapse almost imperceptibly into ' $\overline{oo}$ ' as the voice descends into the lower register: the pressure of breath should also be somewhat relaxed as the voice reaches the lowest notes. Any harshness of tone in individual boys or girls should at once be checked, or the whole choir or chorus may soon be infected. Every lesson or practice should begin

Soft singing. with a few soft and slow exercises, and the pupils should be made to realise that soft singing, sustained at its right pitch, is a sign of good and artistic production. When the ability to sing softly (and at the same time in tune) has been attained, the voices should be trained to increase and decrease the tone gradually on single notes or more extended musical phrases. No finer effect can be produced than a real ' crescendo ' or ' diminuendo,' especially when rendered by a number of voices.

Position of the tongue. The position of the tongue should be observed. It should lie, as far as possible, flat in the mouth. Bad tone is often produced solely by the rising of the tongue, which then interferes with the clear emission of tone from the mouth.

Avoid strain. As in taking breath, so in actual singing, all undue effort should be avoided. The voice should be produced easily at all times. All visible attempts at straining (e.g. rush of blood to the face), especially when the higher notes are being sung, should be stopped promptly. Any contortions of the facial muscles should be noticed and corrected.

Shouting, etc. Finally, choristers, at any rate in a picked choir, must understand that they must share in their choirmaster's care of their voices. Although they need not be debarred from the healthy pleasures that most boys enjoy, they must nevertheless feel that shouting, or any kind of foolish behaviour which produces colds or hoarseness, is particularly to be avoided, since the results in their case are immediately more serious than in the case of boys whose voices are not being specially trained.

CHAPTER VII

EXPRESSION

NOTHING is more important in the musical training of boys and girls than the need of expression. Good singing demands reasonable modulation of the tones of the voice and an intelligent delivery of the words. Both these requirements are attained only by careful training. The first has already been discussed in chapter VI, and exercises bearing on the question will be found at the end of the book. We will now direct our attention to the second point—intelligent delivery of the words.

Voice-modulation. Delivery of words.

Earlier in the book mention was made of the well-known fact that the possession of a beautiful speaking voice is a valuable asset to most people. For all lecturers, preachers, teachers or public speakers, good elocution is of equal, if not greater importance. The foundations of success in this department of daily life should be laid undoubtedly at school. Ordinary conversation (in which one or two persons only are concerned, at close quarters) is usually slipshod : consonants are clipped and slurred, and vowels are seldom pure. To attempt to remedy this is a gigantic if not impossible task. But every boy and girl should learn as soon as possible that, in appealing to a number of people, whether in speaking or singing, success depends almost entirely on every word being heard and understood by the listeners. Good habits in this respect cannot be practised too soon. The teacher may quote or invent sentences shewing how initial and final consonants and aspirates are carelessly elided or mispronounced by untrained people. For example, ' Why *h*op ye so, ye *h*igh *h*ills ? ' ' It is a har*d t*ask to spea*k* *c*learly in u*nn*atura*l l*anguage '; ' Ri*ch*us ' for righ*t*eous ; ' Lore ' for law, etc., etc. The pupils should also realise that short and much-used words such as 'a,' ' an,' ' the,' ' of' etc., become inaudible in a large space unless they are clearly spoken or sung. Further, it is important that choristers, who have constantly to repeat the words of the Liturgy, should utter each word carefully, and make a slight pause between each sentence and the next. In this connection, it is worthy of note that ' monotoning ' in parts of the Liturgy, is less likely to lead to slipshod pronunciation than ordinary speaking.

Words must be understood. The words to be said or sung must be first *understood* by the pupils: otherwise due expression is impossible. The teacher should encourage his pupils to put expression, as they themselves feel it, into the words that they are to sing. As far as possible, therefore, the words should be read aloud before they are sung, if not by all the pupils, at any rate by one or two : the others may then in turn criticise the reader. The teacher meanwhile should note and explain the failures : they will usually be due to the fact that the pupil has failed to get his mouth into the right shape for the different vowels and consonants, or has not used his tongue and lips with enough care. Further, the older pupils must understand that good voice technique (i.e. breathing and pure tone), as well as elocution, is indispensable for a satisfactory rendering of all vocal music. The best composers will be found to have set their words with care : they will have secured the right accents, and will have made the music rise or fall with the corresponding tones of the speaking voice. The varying moods of each song or anthem should be observed and brought out by the singers : here again a complete grasp of the words is essential.

Some people try to maintain that English is an unsatisfactory, or even an impossible, language for singing purposes. Such a view is founded on a misconception. The English language is frequently treated so badly by speakers and singers that it is perhaps not surprising that people who have not studied the question at all deeply may think that the language is at fault, rather than the would-be interpreters. English, like any other language, is impossible to sing unless the singer can first *speak* it properly and also understand the meaning of the words to be sung. (This is at times a difficult task, since the words of a large number of so-called English songs do not appear to have any meaning.) The English language is complicated, inasmuch as it has a great variety of sounds, both of vowels and consonants, which need to be carefully differentiated. It has been said that Italian is especially good for singing purposes, because its vowel sounds are mostly broad and sonorous. There is doubtless some truth in this remark: but it implies that languages which possess vowel sounds, some of which are less sonorous than others, are less fit for singing purposes. Such a view is surely fallacious. The language which can produce the greatest variety of sounds has command of the widest range of expression. Moreover, continual 'sonority,' whether in singing, orchestral playing, or any other branch of musical art, is apt to become monotonous: thin or 'closed' effects form welcome contrasts to breadth and sonority, whether in dramatic or purely lyrical situations. Analogies to this view can be found in the other arts. It is at least probable that a language which served Shakespeare and the English translators of the Bible as a vehicle of expression, will continue to serve poets and musicians in the future. If singing teachers will but impress upon their pupils the need for singing their words exactly as a good *speaker* would deliver them, giving due expression to every word with their minds as well as their voices; and if all singers will determine to sing that music only which is set to good poetry by good composers; we shall then all realise that the English language is not only as good as any other for singing purposes, but also that it has a range of expression equalled by few.

Rhythm.
Folk-songs,
madrigals,
motets, etc.

Another feature of true expression is a grasp of the *rhythm* of both words and music. This factor will not be realised unless the teacher be well read and experienced. Some rhythms, both in poetry and music, are simple and fairly obvious: others are more complicated. Many folk-songs contain unusual rhythms, which need to be pointed out and explained to the pupils. In modal music of the 16th and 17th centuries the rhythms are quite different and distinct from those of later centuries. Some knowledge of the church modes (as they are called), and the use made of them by the earlier composers, is therefore essential. Many folk-songs, as well as the motets and madrigals of the 16th and 17th centuries, are written in these modes: and the differences of tonality as well as of rhythm, compared with most later works, must be pointed out to the pupils. An intelligent explanation of the features of the various modes, and of the more modern major and minor scales, will be found to interest children, and also will enable them to avoid many blunders in reading modal music at sight. Both teacher and pupils must always bear in mind, in dealing with much of the music of the 16th and 17th centuries and also with many folk-songs, that bar-lines were not used when the music in question was invented or written. The bar-lines in such instances have been put in purely for modern convenience, and are intended for the eye rather than the ear: so that frequently it will be wrong to sing according to modern accentuation, giving an accent on the first beat of the bar, and so on. The sense of the passage must always be our guide: if we follow the accents and rhythm of the words, without reference to the bar-lines, we shall be on the way to achieve the right effect.

Rhythms of
hymns.

In this connection it may be well to draw attention to the unintelligent way in which many hymns and hymn-tunes are both written and sung. The rhythms of succeeding verses of the same hymn are often widely different from each other. Often the writer of a hymn and the composer of the tune seem both to have forgotten that each verse of the hymn has to be sung to the same tune. Let us take an instance from a popular hymn—that beginning 'Abide with me...' The first verse begins with the following rhythm: ⌣ – ⌣ –: yet the second verse begins 'Swift to its close...,' where the rhythm is – ⌣ ⌣ –. It is almost impossible that the same tune should fit both these verses; but even so, the composer of the tune has made matters worse by writing a long note for the opening of the tune, which may fit the beginning of the second verse, but makes a ludicrously false accent at the beginning of the first verse. Examples such as this can be multiplied. Another stumbling-block is the fact that many hymn-writers carry on a sentence without any stop from one line to the next. This of course is a feature that obtains in the finest metrical poetry: but in hymns it is a doubtful expedient, unless the hymn-writer be sure of a sympathetic and intelligent composer to set his words to music. In any case it is probable that the average congregation and even the average choir will choose to make nonsense of the words. Let us take another instance from a popular source—the hymn (if it can be properly called a hymn) beginning 'Lead, kindly light...' In the first verse the 5th and 6th lines are:

> Keep Thou my feet; I do not ask to see
> The distant scene: one step enough for me.

Here the writer of the tune has thought fit to sustain for a whole bar the last syllable of the 5th line, thus making it as difficult as possible for even the most intelligent singer to carry on his or her voice into the next line with the sense of the words. The usual result is that choir and congregation take a breath after the word 'see,' and begin an entirely fresh sentence with the words 'The distant scene,' incidentally having to make a strong accent on the short and unimportant word 'The.' It would be far better in this particular case to let the poetry make its personal appeal without publicly singing it. However, as popular sentiment will probably not be baulked, choirmasters will effect something by instructing their choirs to take breath at the stops only, even though the tune does its best to hinder them.

Two typical cases have been quoted to shew how hymn-writers or composers of tunes (especially the latter) have set obstacles in the way of intelligent congregational singing. For the first (the example of different verses having different rhythms) there seems no reasonable remedy. For the second, particularly in less glaring instances than the one quoted, choirs should be instructed always to follow the meaning of the words: if the sense demand that the voice be carried on without a break from the end of one line through the beginning of another, then breath must be taken in the right place to ensure this result. The best congregational hymn-tunes are those which move steadily on with notes of equal value, in 2 or 4 time. Pauses at the ends of lines should in no case be allowed; a fraction of a second for taking breath is all that is needed at any time[1].

Finally, every choir and chorus should understand the importance

---

[1] The pause-marks at the ends of lines in the old German chorales, especially in those harmonized by J. S. Bach, seem to be misunderstood by conductors, choir-masters and congregations. Their origin appears to be doubtful. They may have signified merely the ends of the lines, before bars were introduced. In any case their modern application can be, at the most, but a taking of breath between the different sections of the melody. To make a lengthy pause on the last syllable of every line, as do most conductors and organists in their rendering of the chorales in Bach's settings of the Passion and elsewhere, is to distort the rhythm of the words and music, and to make an unimportant note or syllable unduly prominent. Further, a careful examination of the more elaborate settings of the old tunes by J. S. Bach, both in the Passions and in the choral preludes for organ, will convince any unbiassed observer that in many cases the pause-marks (which Bach still retained, even in his instrumental versions) could not mean a 'wait' on the last note of each line of the tune; since elaborate counterpoint against the original melody, often in scale-motion, runs continuously through a whole movement, and to wait on any note of the original tune would mean a ludicrous holding-up of the accompanying counterpoint, often in the middle of a musical sentence.

both of beginning and ending all their phrases together. When a Beginnings and endings of phrases. conductor is present, the matter is simple, if the chorus attend to the conductor's beat. But in the case of a church choir, where there is usually no one to indicate the time except the organist at the keyboard, the singers should get into the habit of holding notes for their exact value, especially at the end of a phrase. If there be a pause on the last note, it is well that the choirmaster should indicate at practice-time how much longer than its face value (e.g. double, or half as long again) he wishes the note to be held. All rests should be observed scrupulously. If a composer has put rests instead of notes, obviously he intended them to be kept. A solo singer possibly may, without bad effect, prolong or shorten a note at will: but where a number of singers are concerned, any arbitrary lengthening or shortening of notes can only result in 'ragged' singing, and consequent loss of true expression.

CHAPTER VIII

SINGING OUT OF TUNE

In chapter I, it was stated that singing is an art and must be carefully taught, and that so-called 'natural' singing does not carry the singer far. As an illustration we may cite the well-known fact that choirs and choruses which receive but little or indifferent training are very prone to sing out of tune—usually flat. It is true that this fault is by no means unknown in highly-trained choirs: but it is in the belief that by good training a cure can be found in nearly every case that the causes and remedies will be discussed in this chapter.

It is assumed, first of all, that no choir or chorus will contain for long any boys or girls who have musically-defective ears: that is, every would-be singer must be able[1] to produce any given sound at any moment, and must also be able to recognise the fact that he is singing

[1] See chapter IV, pages xviii and xix.

out of tune when it is pointed out to him. Without these safeguards all the labours of the choirmaster may be useless.

The chief causes of singing out of tune are :

Forcing of tone (too much breath), especially in the lower part of the voice. This produces both flat and sharp singing.

Physical weariness. }
Ill-health. } These usually produce flat singing.
Laziness. }

All these defects are, or should be, temporary, and so may be cured. The whole question of good tone-production and the evils of forcing the voice were discussed in chapter VI (q.v.). Flat singing is a far more common phenomenon than singing sharp. The latter, which is far harder to cure, can be assigned usually to one of two causes. First, it is sometimes found that a boy or girl, through possessing a defective ear, sings sharp without knowing it, and does not recognise the fault even when it is pointed out. This does not necessarily happen on single notes, so that the initial test mentioned above does not always reveal the evil: but the voice gets gradually sharper in the course of the singing, usually as it mounts into the higher register. Cases of this kind are generally hopeless, and boys or girls with such a tendency must be removed from the choir or chorus.

Sharp singing.

Again, a habit of forcing too much breath through the larynx will produce sharp as well as flat singing. In the one case, too much breath makes the voice sharp, just as overblowing a wind instrument raises the pitch. In the other, the muscles of the larynx, being forced, suddenly relax owing to the strain, and the pitch sinks with the loss of tension. The cure in either case is proper management of the breath (see chapter VI).

Physical weariness.

Physical weariness will often produce flat singing. The teacher must take care that his pupils are not overworked or put to any undue strain. Reference to chapter V on 'length of practice,' both with regard to choirs and school choruses, will be helpful here.

If a boy or girl is unwell and still tries to join in the vocal practice, Ill-health. it is likely that flat singing will result. At any time the exercise of the voice means some mental and physical effort, and this necessary effort becomes irksome or even impossible when the pupil's bodily and mental energies are below the normal. It is not suggested that every little ailment should receive disproportionate consideration from the teacher: for both teacher and pupil alike often have to work against physical odds. But the singing-hour should be a pleasant diversion from other studies, and no pupil should be forced to sing when the effort involved seems too great. Listless (and therefore flat) singing will probably follow, and the other pupils may be infected.

In connection with the health of the pupils, the teacher is urgently Light and advised to see that the practice-room is well lighted and ventilated. ventilation. Every boy and girl should be able to see clearly the notes and words which they are required to read, whether from a book or a blackboard. Also fresh, pure air is essential for good singing. Vitiated air, or an atmosphere that is either too hot or too cold, will unfailingly produce bad singing.

Another cause of flat singing is laziness. It is unnecessary to Laziness. suggest remedies for this fault: but experience tells us that boys and girls are seldom lazy if their work be interesting and varied. It should be the teacher's care to see that the practice does not become dull and perfunctory: otherwise retribution will be swift and certain for teacher and pupils alike.

It sometimes happens that flat singing persists in a choir or chorus Monotoning and hum- in spite of the most anxious efforts of the teacher. If all the recom- ming. mendations here put forward have been tried without complete success, it is suggested that recitation of words on a soft monotone and 'humming' (i.e. holding sustained notes with the mouth closed) be tried as remedies.

CHAPTER IX

THE APPROACH OF PUBERTY

IN due course puberty will assert itself in the life of every boy and girl, and the vocal apparatus, in the case of boys at any rate, will undergo considerable changes. This problem demands the most serious care and thought from every choirmaster or teacher of school singing. Much has been written on this subject, and medical authorities as well as voice-trainers have expressed divergent views as to whether girls and boys should be allowed to sing or not at this period of their lives. On the whole, the evidence seems to point to the conclusion that it is unwise probably for a girl, and almost certainly for a boy, to sing at such a time. As the cases of girls and boys are somewhat different, it will be convenient to consider the two sexes separately, beginning with the boys.

Boys. At the advent of puberty in boys, the treble voice slowly (sometimes very rapidly) disappears, and the adult voice begins to assert itself. **Alto, tenor and bass voices at puberty.** Occasionally the pitch of the voice sinks but little, and the true male alto voice appears: such cases are comparatively rare. Somewhat oftener a tenor voice gradually forms, the pitch dropping about an octave. The commonest case of all is when the treble voice changes to a baritone (sometimes bass). Here the pitch falls about an octave and a half, and the change is usually more rapid than in the other **Age of puberty.** instances quoted. The age at which the voice thus 'breaks' is variable. Sometimes it is as early as 13, at other times as late as 17 or even later. Usually, however, puberty makes its appearance between the ages of 14 and 16, and it is at about that age, therefore, that boys in choirs or school choruses should cease to sing treble.

Now it must be obvious, when, in a comparatively short time, a voice sinks an octave or more in pitch, that some considerable changes must be taking place in the larynx. It is unnecessary to discuss the medical aspect of the matter in these pages, beyond stating that all authorities are agreed, that during the bodily changes involved in the approach of puberty, the boy's whole vocal apparatus is in an abnormal and delicate state, and should therefore be treated with the utmost care. As soon as the first signs of 'breaking' appear, the boy should at once cease to sing entirely, until his man's voice asserts itself unmistakably. The whole change may take a few months, or even a year or more. But however short or long the period may be, it cannot be too strongly urged that the wisest and kindest course is to insist on complete rest for the singing voice. It is doubtless a temptation to some choirmasters to keep boys at their singing work during the 'breaking' period. The boys in question are usually the oldest and most experienced of the choristers, and not infrequently their voices are in parts exceptionally brilliant at such a time. But the boy's future singing (and speaking) voice is probably at stake. His treble voice, at the most, will last eight or nine years; whereas his adult voice has to serve him for the rest of his life.

Changes in the vocal apparatus.

Complete abstinence from singing.

The symptoms of 'breaking' are easily detected. The lower or the upper notes begin to disappear: or particular notes, formerly clear and true, become uncertain: or occasionally the voice will 'crack' and fly off, usually on a high note. A day or two will suffice for the teacher to determine if these signs are caused merely by a cold: if not, the boy in question should be superseded, and should be told to rest his singing voice entirely, and his speaking voice as much as possible (certainly from shouting), until his adult voice appears in due strength and proper quality.

Symptoms of 'breaking.'

The change in the actual vocal apparatus of a girl at the approach of puberty obviously is not of the same kind or so considerable as in the case of the average boy. The pitch of the girl's voice alters but little, if at all, at such a time. Occasionally the mezzo-soprano voice

Girls.

sinks into a contralto (a drop or increase of a 5th at the most), but this is uncommon. Some famous women singers have sung right through the puberty period until late in life without any apparent harm resulting to their voices. It seems safer, however, to let the voice rest as soon as puberty appears, i.e. at about 14 years of age. In most cases it will be unwise to train a girl's voice for solo singing until about the age of 17.

Training for boys and girls after the puberty period.   Both sexes will need further training when once the adult voice has become settled. The young man's voice especially will need careful supervision. The altered condition of the adult voice (especially in the case of a baritone or a bass) will mean a different physical and mental outlook. This implies a complete change from the vocal point of view also. The same argument, from the purely physical point of view, applies equally to young women.

CHAPTER X

SELECTION OF MUSIC

A FEW suggestions will now be put forward as to the selection of music for performance, both with regard to schools and also choirs. Let us consider first the case of those schools which possess a chapel, or at any rate a school hall, in which congregational services will be held regularly.

Unison singing during service-time.   In girls' schools the singing during service-time, whether there be a choir or not, should be mainly in unison. Contralto voices are rare amongst school-girls, certainly before the age of puberty. The majority of the voices will be mezzo-soprano ; and, provided the compass of the music to be sung in unison be about ♮, it will be found that practically all girls who have voices can join in without effort. In two-part music (unless it be written for sopranos and mezzo-sopranos, without contraltos) the higher voices will outnumber the lower; in three-part music, which is usually written for sopranos, mezzo-sopranos and contraltos, the middle part (mezzo-sopranos) will drown the other two.

In boys' schools, similarly, the singing should be mostly in unison and octaves. Those boys who have not reached the age of puberty should sing treble, and those whose voices have fully settled for some time after the advent of puberty should sing an octave below the trebles. There is a pernicious tendency in our boys' public schools to obtain four-part harmony for service and concert purposes by making some boys sing alto and others tenor. In nearly every case there is a serious risk of such alto and tenor singers having their voices irretrievably ruined. The real alto and tenor voices are rare amongst school-boys, and the voices of the boys thus requisitioned are usually in the transitional state which immediately precedes and follows the coming of puberty—a period when the voice should be rested as much as possible[1] (see chapter IX). *Altos and tenors in boys' schools.*

It is of grave importance then that alto and tenor voice parts should not be thought of in school chapels, unless those parts can be taken almost entirely by masters or members of the staff whose voices are mature. Unison singing in a school chapel is usually far more majestic and impressive than four-part harmony, especially when the two middle parts of the latter are sung by a handful of people, some of whom at

[1] Occasionally a boy's voice, after breaking early, settles gently into a real alto or tenor before the age of 18 : but even so, voices so rare should not be expected to sing their part against the large mass of trebles and baritones which form the bulk of the usual school choir or chorus. They should be carefully trained, if possible, away from the rest.

At Oxford and Cambridge about twenty scholarships are given annually for tenor and bass (sometimes alto) voices. The large majority of these scholarships are offered by various colleges at Cambridge, and are won usually by boys who are leaving school for the University. Their value ranges from £30 to £90 a year.

least ought not to be singing at all. The careful choirmaster will see that the music to be sung in unison is kept as a rule within the following

limits : . This compass will be suitable for the ordinary

treble voice, and also (an octave lower) will be fairly within the range of the ordinary baritone, which is the commonest adult male voice, at any rate in England[1].

Singing of secular songs, etc.

All that has been written regarding the music at service-time applies with equal force to the selection of secular music for school purposes. Unison songs should be the rule, for boys or girls. When two-part songs are used, the second voice should not be at a lower pitch throughout than the first voice. Both parts should have about the same compass: otherwise one set of voices will be constantly singing in their lower register, and will probably force their tone. Also the upper and more beautiful register, at any rate of the boy's voice, will thus be

Canons, catches and rounds. National songs.

neglected. Canons, catches and rounds are the best forms of part-music for school purposes. As regards unison songs, the teacher may easily find suitable material in the admirable books of national songs now edited specially for schools, both in tonic sol-fa and in staff notation. Here he is on firm ground: words and music have stood the test of time—the surest critic. For every teacher should make it his first care to see that only the best forms of art (however simple) are studied by the classes under his control, as regards both the words and the music. Songs of varied character should be chosen, and the pupils invited to bring out in their singing the salient features (rhythm, expression, etc.) of both music and words.

'Advanced' examples for unison singing.

One or two examples of music suitable for well-trained treble voices to sing in unison are printed at the end of the book, after the vocal exercises. They will be found to provide admirable practice for breathing,

[1] See Appendix, page xlv.

phrasing and flexibility. The six-part Rota or Round, 'Summer is a-coming in' (according to the late Mr Rockstro, by many years the oldest example of part music in existence) will probably be found both interesting and instructive. It is here assigned to 4 treble voices and 2 drone parts underneath: the latter may be sung by adult voices or played on the pianoforte.

Boys who sing in cathedral or church choirs should be encouraged to **Choirs.** sing secular music, whenever time can be found for it. Otherwise they are liable to become narrow in their musical outlook, owing to the constant singing of church music only, especially in the continued repetition of the church canticles. National songs, canons, rounds, etc., will form useful contrasts to anthems, psalms and settings of the church service.

CHAPTER XI

EXERCISES

THE second part of the book consists of a number of exercises designed to meet all the requirements of vocal technique for boys and girls. They have been arranged as far as possible in order of difficulty in each department (keys and times, scales, intervals, flexibility, semitones, sustained notes, syncopation, shakes and turns, phrasing and expression, etc.).

Accompaniments have been provided for the teacher. They are **Accompani-ments to the exercises.** simple, and do not as a rule reduplicate the vocal melody. It is as well to accustom all pupils from the beginning to rely on their eyes and not their ears only, particularly when reading at sight. The accompaniments, therefore, merely supply a slight harmonic basis for the melody. The **Books for pupils only.** vocal part of the exercises (and of the special solos to be sung in unison) are reprinted in a smaller volume, intended for the use of the pupils, either to be held in the hand or placed upon desks. The exercises **Singing with-out accom-paniment.** should be sung sometimes without accompaniment, and the key-note, or the note on which the voices finish, struck at the end of the exercise. Should the voices be then flat or sharp, the exercise should be repeated, still without accompaniment, and the teacher should notice carefully at what moments the boys or girls deviate from the right pitch: he should then correct them, either at the end of the exercise, or by playing a note here and there during the singing, at moments when they are out of tune. In such cases the teacher should be able to explain to the pupils the reasons for their being out of tune.

Beginning on the upper notes. In accordance with the views expressed in chapter VI, most of the exercises begin in the upper register of the voice, especially when they are in sequential form. The pupils must be taught to take the highest note (usually the first) clearly and 'cleanly,' with a forward production, and to carry the same production downwards to the lowest note. As the notes descend, the pressure of breath should gradually be lessened, so as to minimize the chances of forcing the lowest notes, and so avoid coarseness or singing out of tune.

Exercises founded on special difficulties. The teacher may himself invent exercises, in sequential form, out of passages in the music that is being studied, which are melodically or rhythmically difficult: in this way the difficulty is made clear, and impressed on the minds of the pupils by its repetition on different degrees of the scale.

Begin with scales, etc. Scales and vocal exercises should come at the beginning of the practice-hour, for several reasons. First, it is well to get the voices clear and, so to speak, 'lubricated,' before the songs or anthems are taken: for the latter have words, expression and so forth to be taken into account, as well as vocal technique. Again, the pupils may not have been using their singing voices, or may have been shouting, just before the practice-hour. In either case a few scales and well-chosen exercises, especially if sung softly, will bring the voices into a proper condition within a few minutes, provided they be sung with intelligence and care: regular and systematic breathing also will be re-established.

Finally, if the exercises be chosen with reference to the faults Reference to the previous practice. displayed during the previous practice, the teacher can thus drive home the lessons to be learnt from the day or week before, as the case may be. He will often find it useful to spend a minute or two in the middle of the practice on an exercise chosen to illustrate a particular fault.

It is hoped that all the exercises in this book will be found to be of use : but experience suggests that special attention will usually be needed for those involving scale movement (difference of tones and semitones) and diatonic and chromatic intervals, whether small or wide.

APPENDIX

As the contention put forward on pages xli and xlii, with regard to unison singing in boys' public schools, may seem to strike athwart the progress of school singing, which of late years has been admirably fostered by many of those who are in charge of public school music, a scheme is now suggested to supplement the earlier argument.

If unison and octave singing be not enough to satisfy the aspirations of school music at all times (a quite intelligible view from the school standpoint), why should not composers be interested in the problem, and be induced to set good poetry to music to suit the varied require-ments of different public schools ? Some of the finest music has been inspired by 'occasions,' and has been carefully composed to suit the means that each occasion could provide. As an instance of the growth of a special kind of composition we may mention the music written by our best modern composers for women's voices only, largely to meet the requirements of women's choruses, especially in girls' schools and women's colleges. Now some of our younger British composers are in direct touch with public schools, and could hardly serve their generation better than by devoting some of their creative energy to the advancement of the higher branches of school music. Works might be composed for chorus with instrumental accompaniment to suit all needs. The main point would be that the choral parts would have to be written for *trebles* and *baritones of limited range.* It is hardly necessary to point out that two-part writing (especially for chorus) can be made extremely effective. Occasional contrast could be provided by doubling the trebles (particularly if the parts were written in accordance with the view expressed on page xlii concerning two-part songs), and by subdividing the adult voices into baritones and basses; parts for solo voices might also be introduced. Instrumental accompaniment might be written for pianoforte, or for pianoforte and strings, or for any combination of instruments that might be available. If once this idea were taken up, it would not be difficult to find publishers who would see in such a scheme possibilities of success from the business point of view.

EXERCISES.

Exercises **1- 11** illustrate the more usual time-signatures and key-signatures.
The full description of each time– and key-signature should be given by one of the
pupils before the exercise is sung. The rhythm (e.g. "4-bar rhythm, 3 times repeated")
should also be understood in each case.
The sign '⸜⸝'= take breath.
The teacher will decide at what pace the various exercises are to be sung: this will
vary according to circumstances.

6.

7.

MAJOR SCALES.

Exercises **12–37** should be sung slowly (M.M. ♩=60) without portamento, yet smoothly. The teacher should take care that the voices are quite *steady* throughout, and that the exact relations between the whole tones and semitones of the scale are preserved.

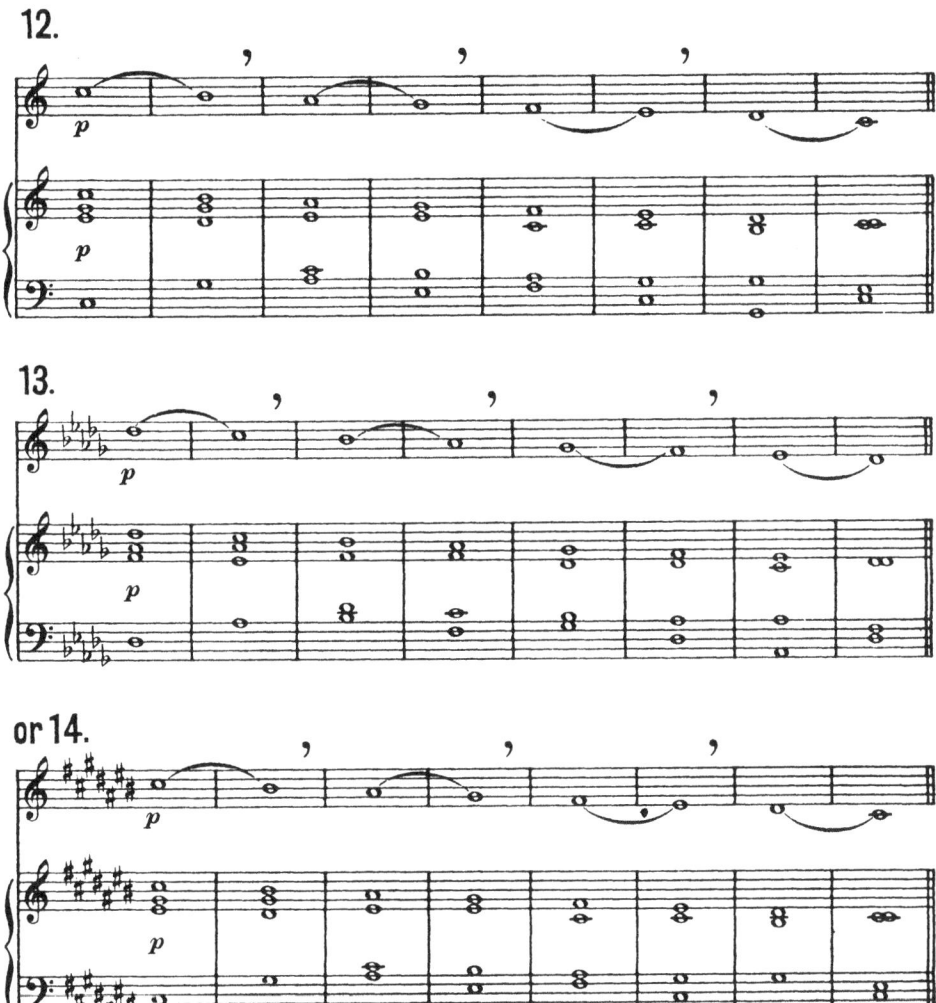

MAJOR SCALES.

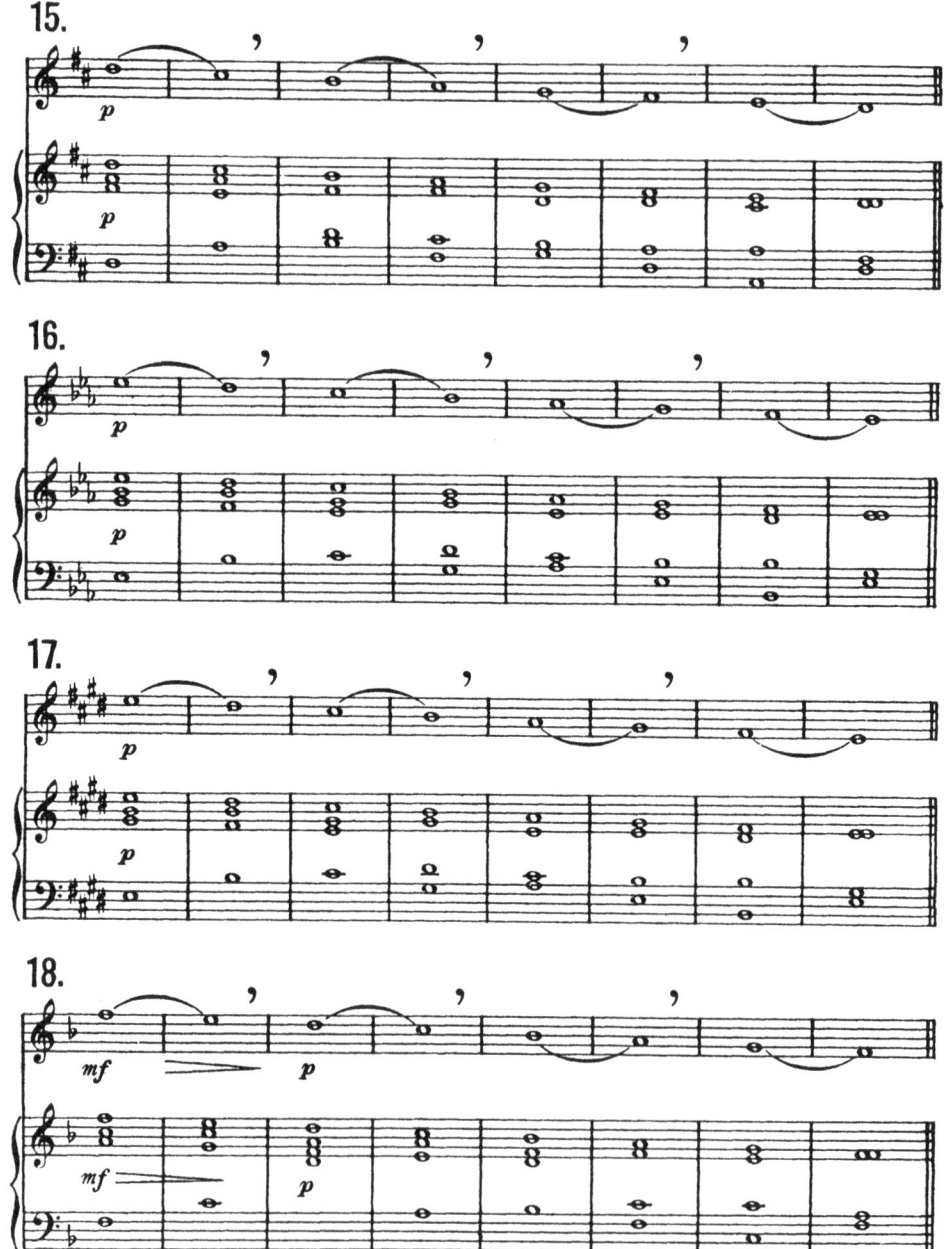

Exercises **23 & 24** should be used solely for boys, and for those boys only who receive regular and constant training.

or 27.

28.

29.

30.

35.

Exercises 36 & 37 should be used solely for boys, and for those boys only who receive regular and constant training.

36.

37.

38.(M.M. ♩ = about 80.)

ARPEGGIOS.

The teacher must see that the pupils carry the head voice down to the lowest note, and also that they do not force the chest voice up in returning to the highest note. The last note in each case must be taken off sharply by merely stopping the breath. The shape of the mouth must not be altered until after the sound has ceased: otherwise a consonant (such as 'm') will be heard at the finish.

39. (M.M. ♩ = 60)

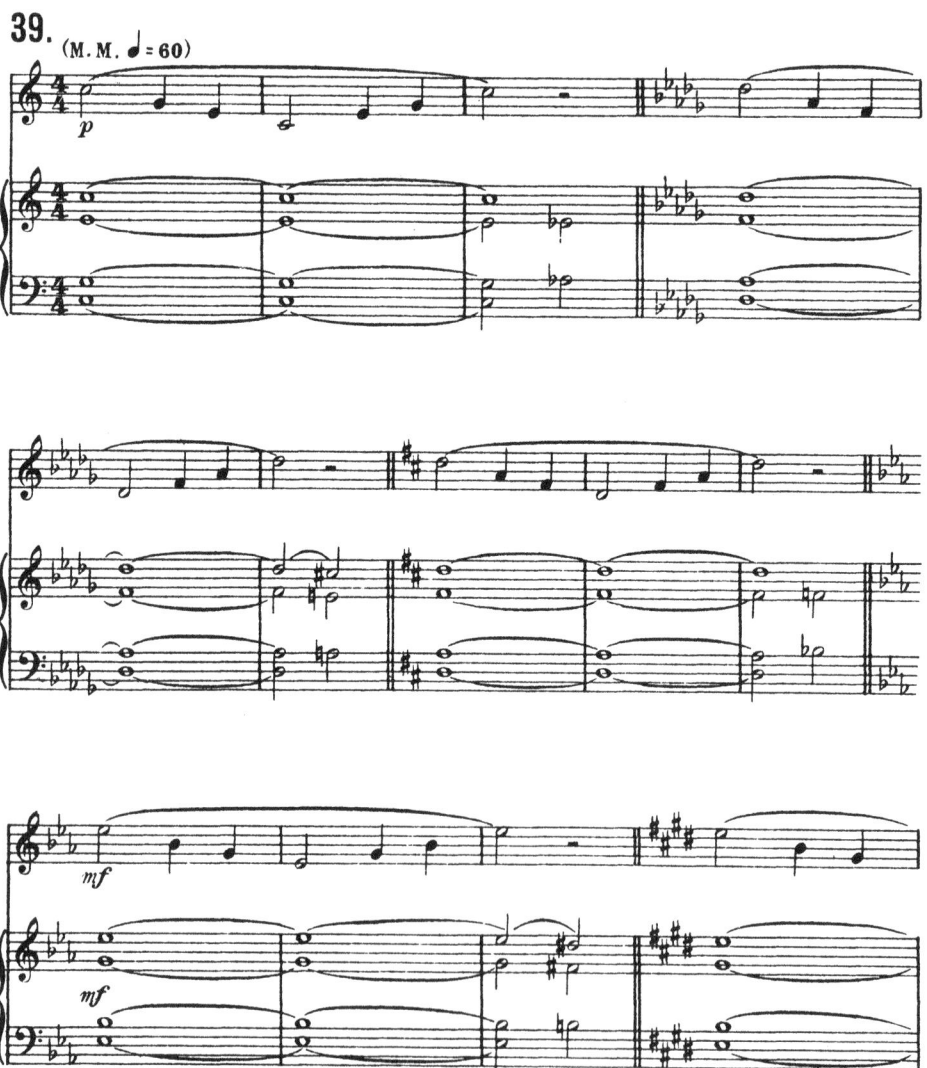

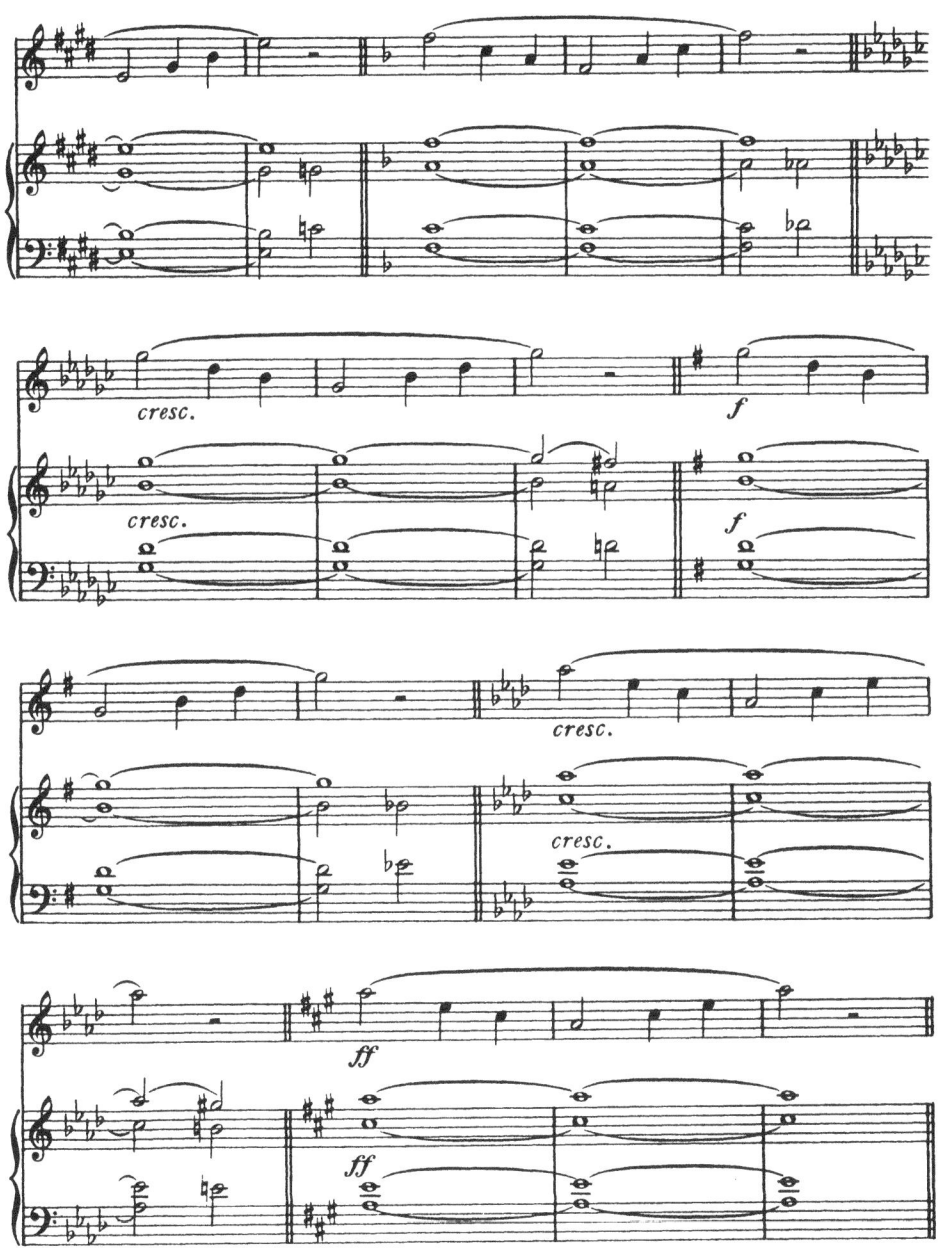

LEAP OF A TENTH.

The leap of a tenth must be made 'cleanly', without a trace of any intermediate note: at the same time the breath must be continuous for each phrase. In singing a wide interval *upwards*, the pupil must take care that the tongue lies flat in the mouth.

19

MINOR SCALES.

Harmonic minor scales. The teacher should make sure that all the pupils clearly understand the difference between the harmonic and melodic forms of the minor scale.

See directions for Ex: 39.

42. (M.M. ♩=92)

Melodic minor scales. These should be practised at the same time as the preceding scales. (Ex: 42)

43.

Exercises on minor scales. These are intended for practice in conjunction with ex: **41-43.**

44. (Harmonic minor.)

45. (Melodic minor.)

INTERVALS.

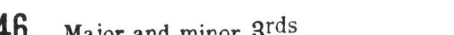

46. Major and minor 3rds.
(M.M. ♩=96)

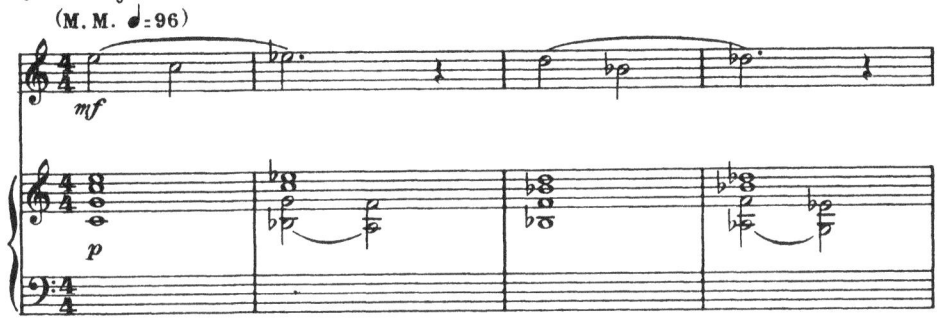

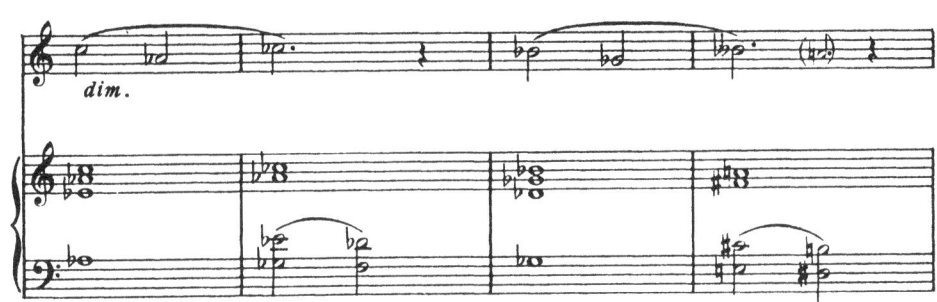

47.   Perfect 4ths.

48. Diatonic 4ths (all in one key.)

49. Perfect and augmented 4ths.

50. Perfect 5<u>ths</u> and perfect 4<u>ths</u>.

51.

54. Minor 7ths and major 6ths.

55. Octaves and major 7ths

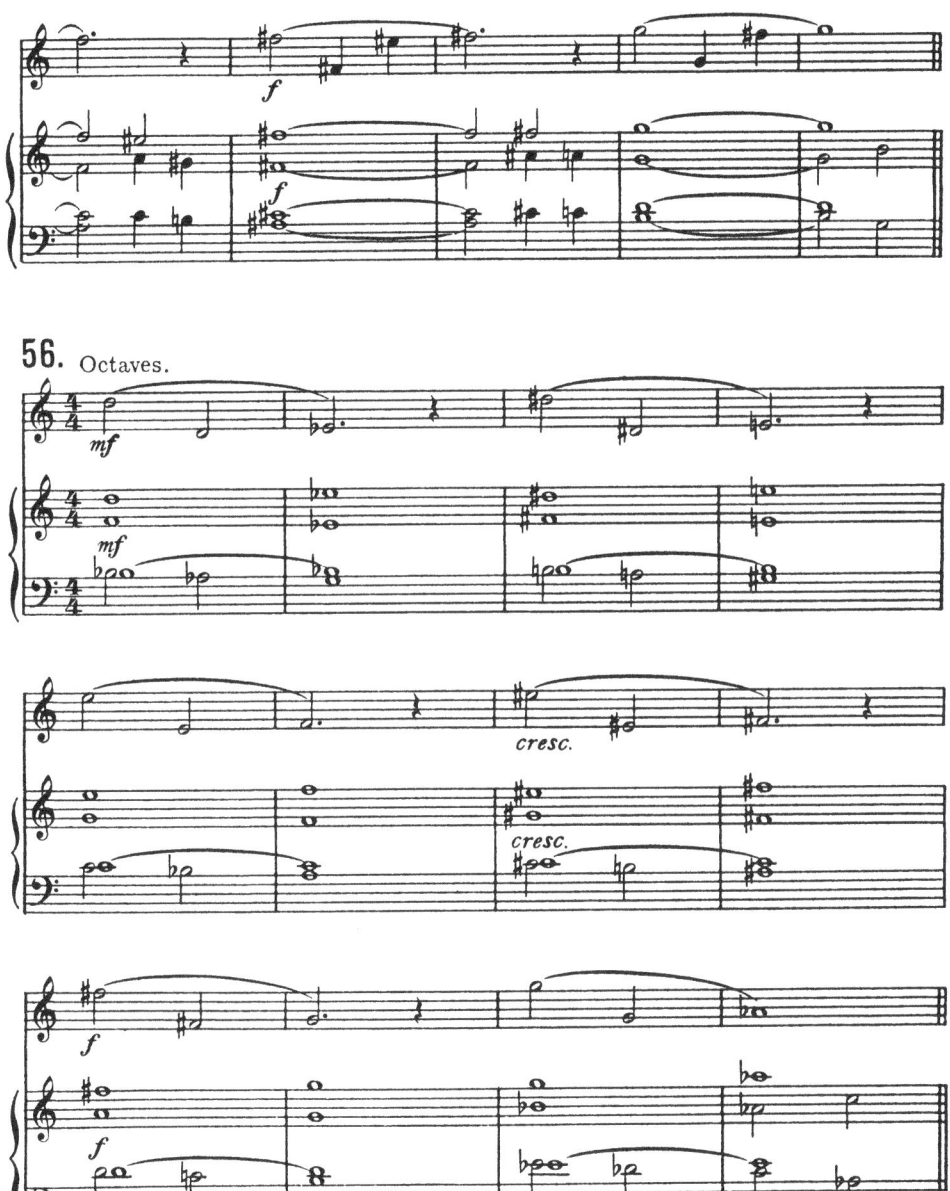

56. Octaves.

57.

EXERCISES FOR FLEXIBILITY.

Exercises 58–64 may be taken somewhat slowly at first, then gradually faster: every note, however, must always be distinct.

58.

FLEXIBILITY.

60.

61.

FLEXIBILITY.

64.

SEMITONES.

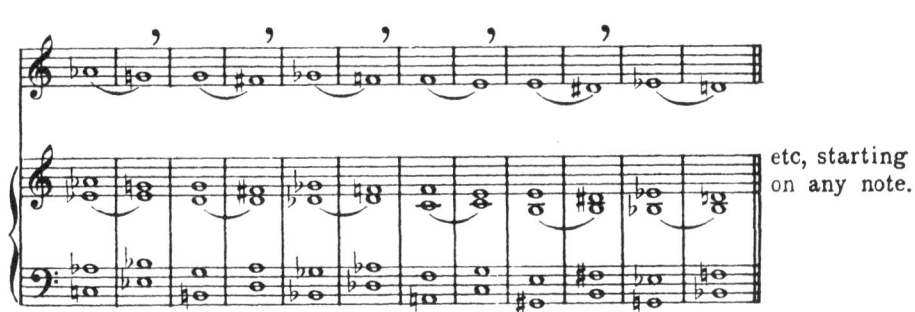

etc, starting on any note.

The teacher will probably find that the tendency of the pupils will be to make the intervals too wide in descending, (and so end flat,) and not wide enough in ascending (with a similar result.)

This and the following exercise had better be sung without accompaniment.

The teacher can put in an occasional chord when necessary.

67.

68.

SHAKES.

This exercise(for shakes and trills) should be practised as fast as a clear enunciation of every demi-semiquaver allows.

69

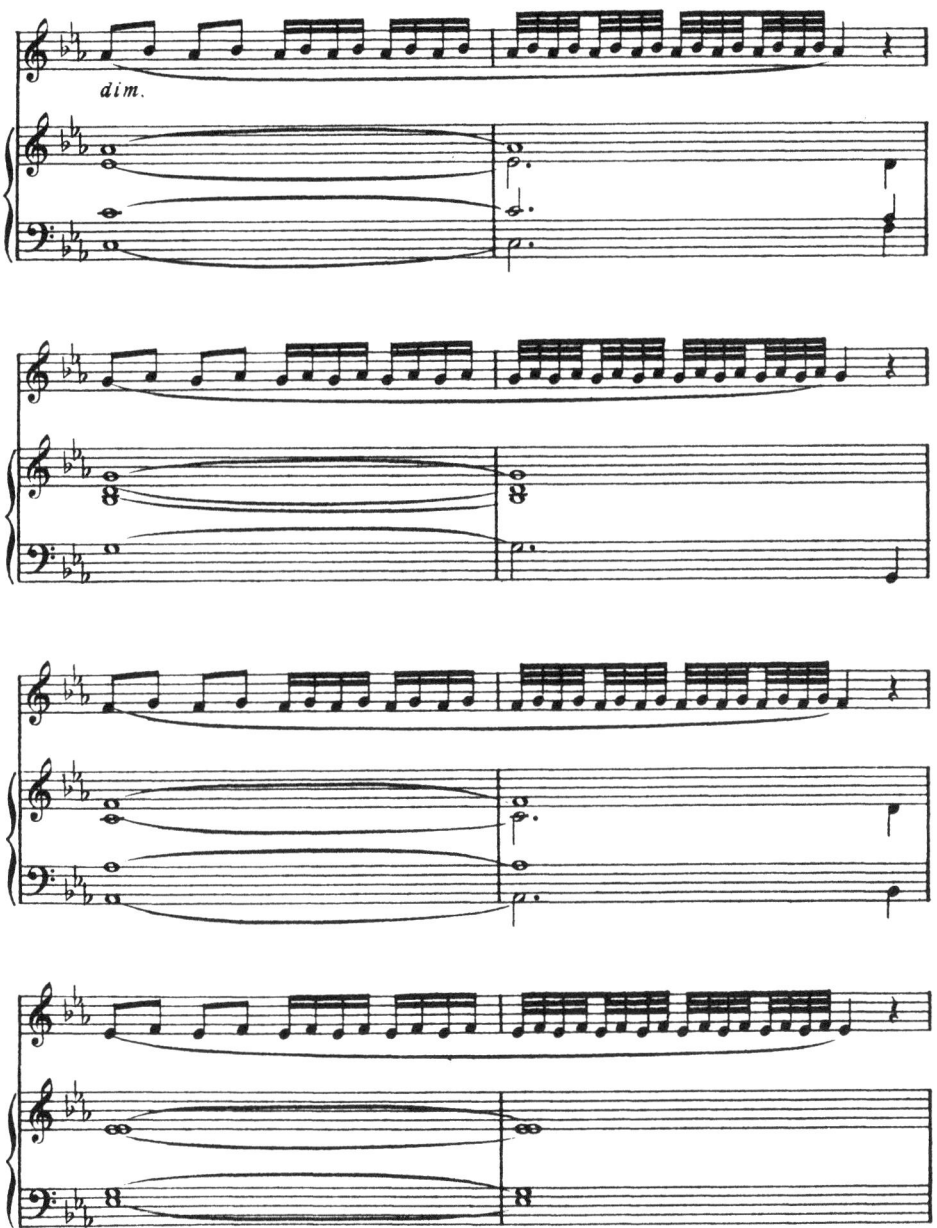

TURNS.

On the 'Turn.' This exercise may be practised either slowly or rapidly.

70.

CRESCENDO AND DIMINUENDO.

For practising *crescendo* and *diminuendo*. The teacher should notice that the main difficulty is in the last 2 bars in each case – i.e. the *gradual* softening of the tone.

71. (M.M. ♩ = 80.)

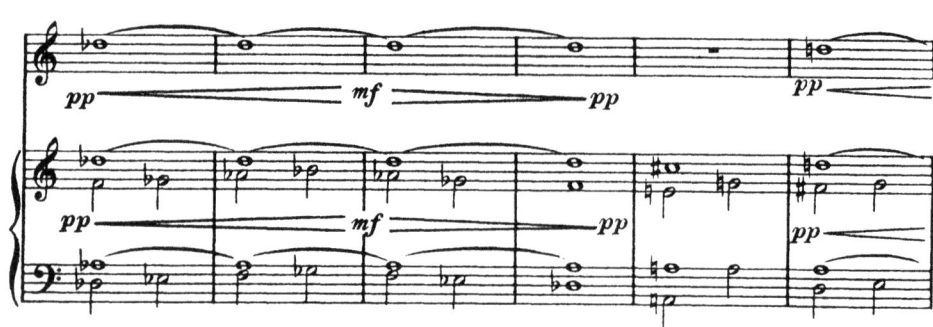

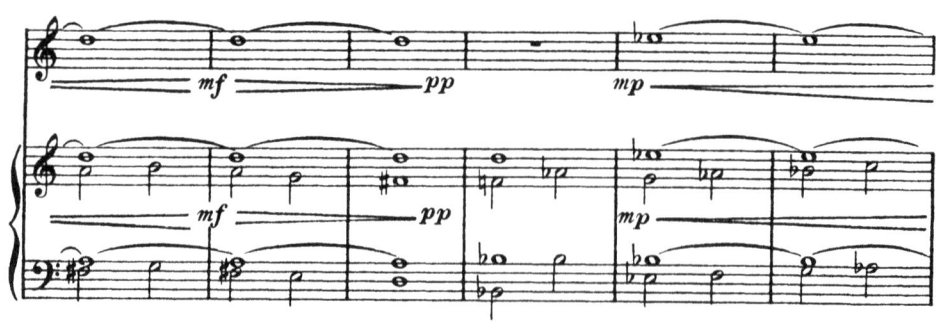

On 'Syncopation'.
72. (M.M. ♩ = 72.)

MODULATION.

In Exercises 74 and 75 the pupils should be questioned on the modulations.   They should find out for themselves what keys are passed through, and at what point each modulation takes place; also what means (chromatic notes, chords etc.) are employed in each instance.

74.

75.

PHRASING AND EXPRESSION.

77.

78.

NYMPHS AND SHEPHERDS.

Song from Purcell's "Libertine."
(The accompaniment arranged from a ms: in the
Fitzwilliam Museum, Cambridge, by B.C. Jones.)

LET THE BRIGHT SERAPHIM.

From Handel's "Samson"
(printed by kind permission of Messrs. Novello & Co)

loud   up - lift - ed   An - gel - trum - pets blow,

LAUDATE DOMINUM.*

(from "Vesperae de Confessore.")

Mozart.

Andante ma un poco sostenuto.

Pianoforte.

* The original movement is for soprano solo and chorus.

Quo - ni - am con - fir - ma - ta est su - per nos mi - se - ri - cor - di - a e - jus, et ve - ri - tas,

★ Some bars of the original have been omitted here.

LAUDATE DOMINUM.

(from "Vesperae de Dominica.")

Mozart.

LAUDATE DOMINUM.

in _____ prin - ci - pi - o   et nunc et ___ sem - per   et

nunc _____ et _____ sem -

a - men, a - - men.

SUMMER IS A-COMING IN.
A ROTA, OR ROUND.

Composed *circa* A.D. 1226.

Edited by W. S. ROCKSTRO.

(Printed by kind permission of Messrs. Novello & Co:)

NOTE.— There is good ground for believing that "Sumer is icumen in" is by many years the oldest example of part-music in existence. For a full account of the original MS., transcribed by John of Fornsete, a monk of the Monastery of Reading, about the year 1226, and now in the British Museum (Harleian MSS., No. 978) see Sir G. Grove's "Dictionary of Music and Musicians," vol. iii., pp. 268-270. The Round may be sung either by four Trebles and two Tenors (or Basses), or by four Tenors and two Basses; in either case without instrumental accompaniment.—W. S. R.

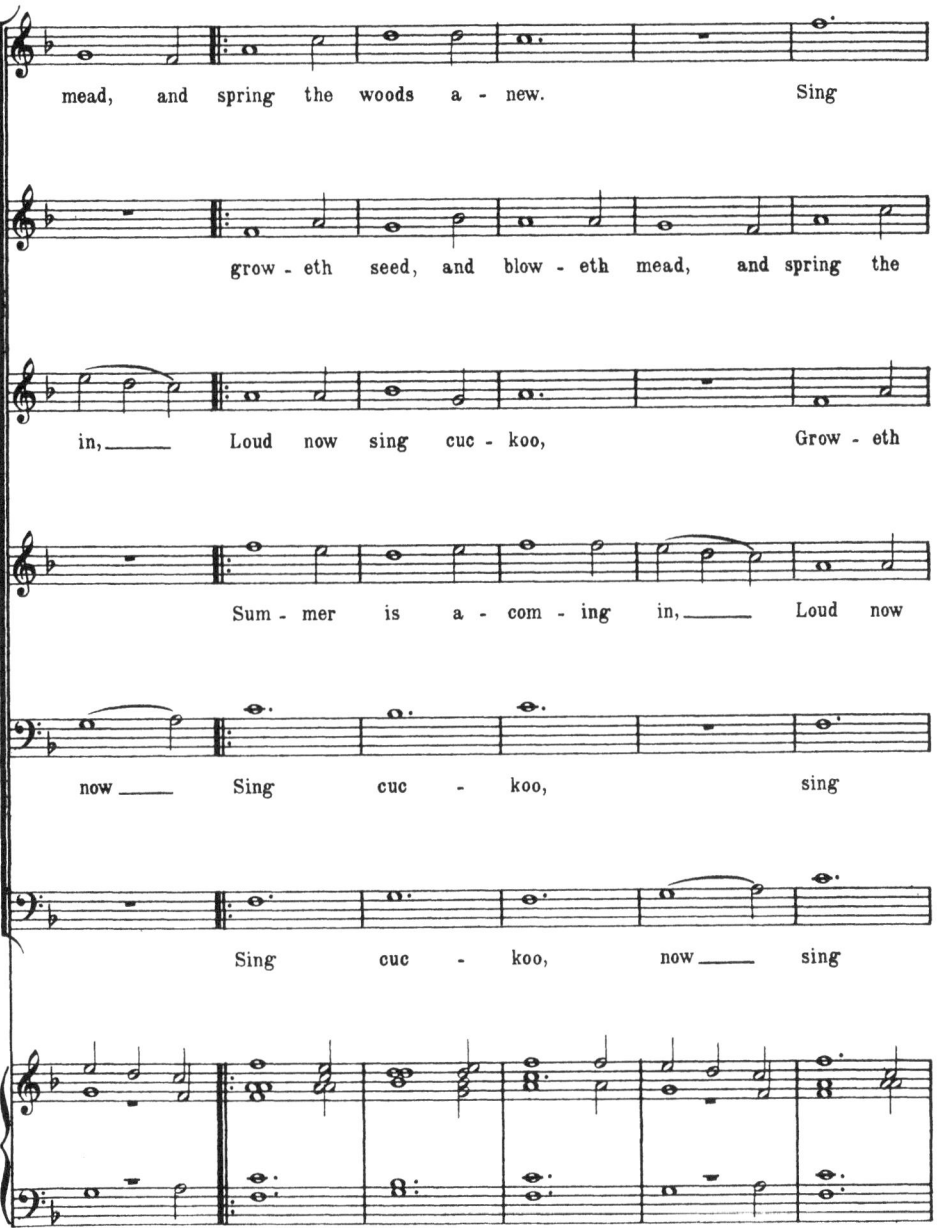

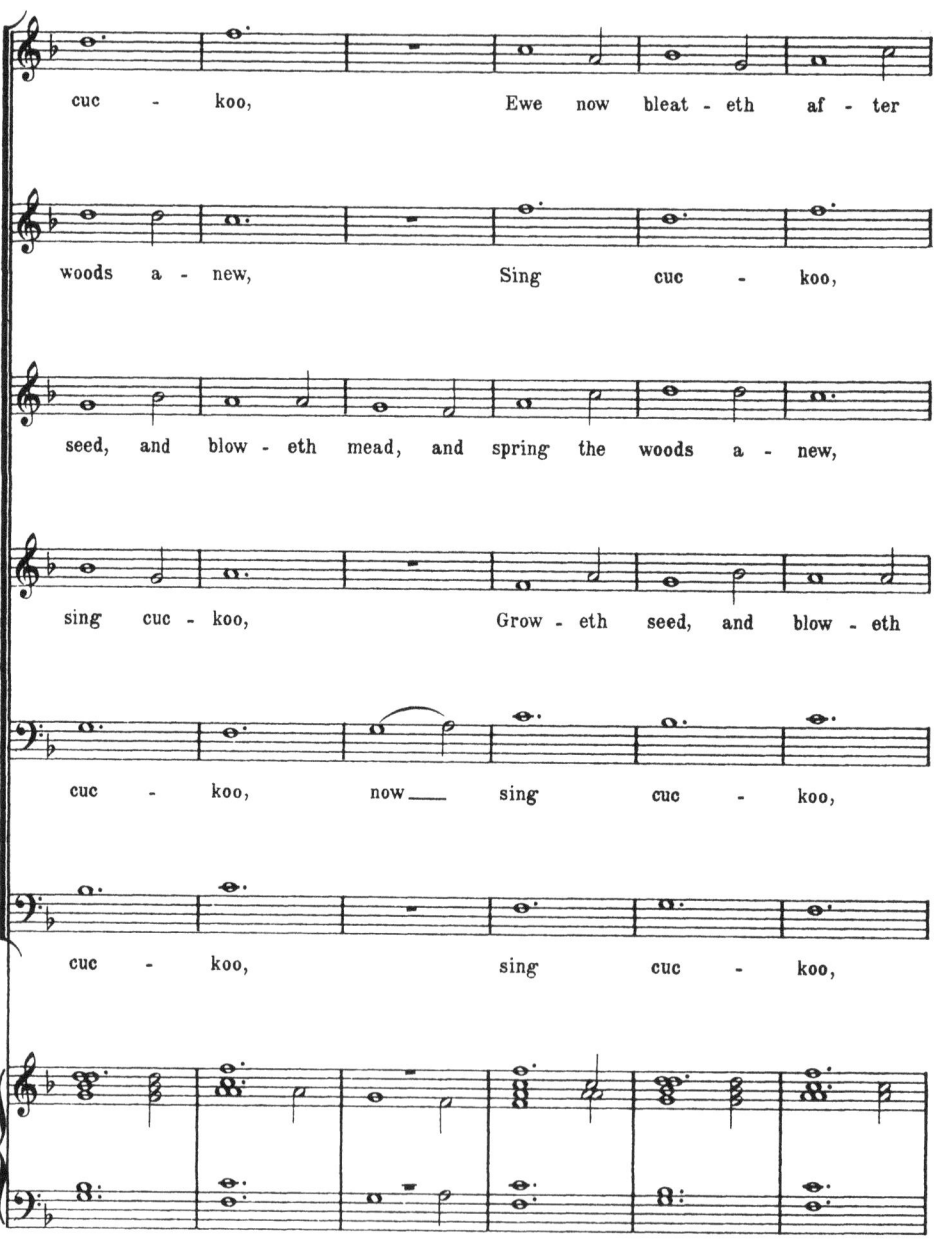

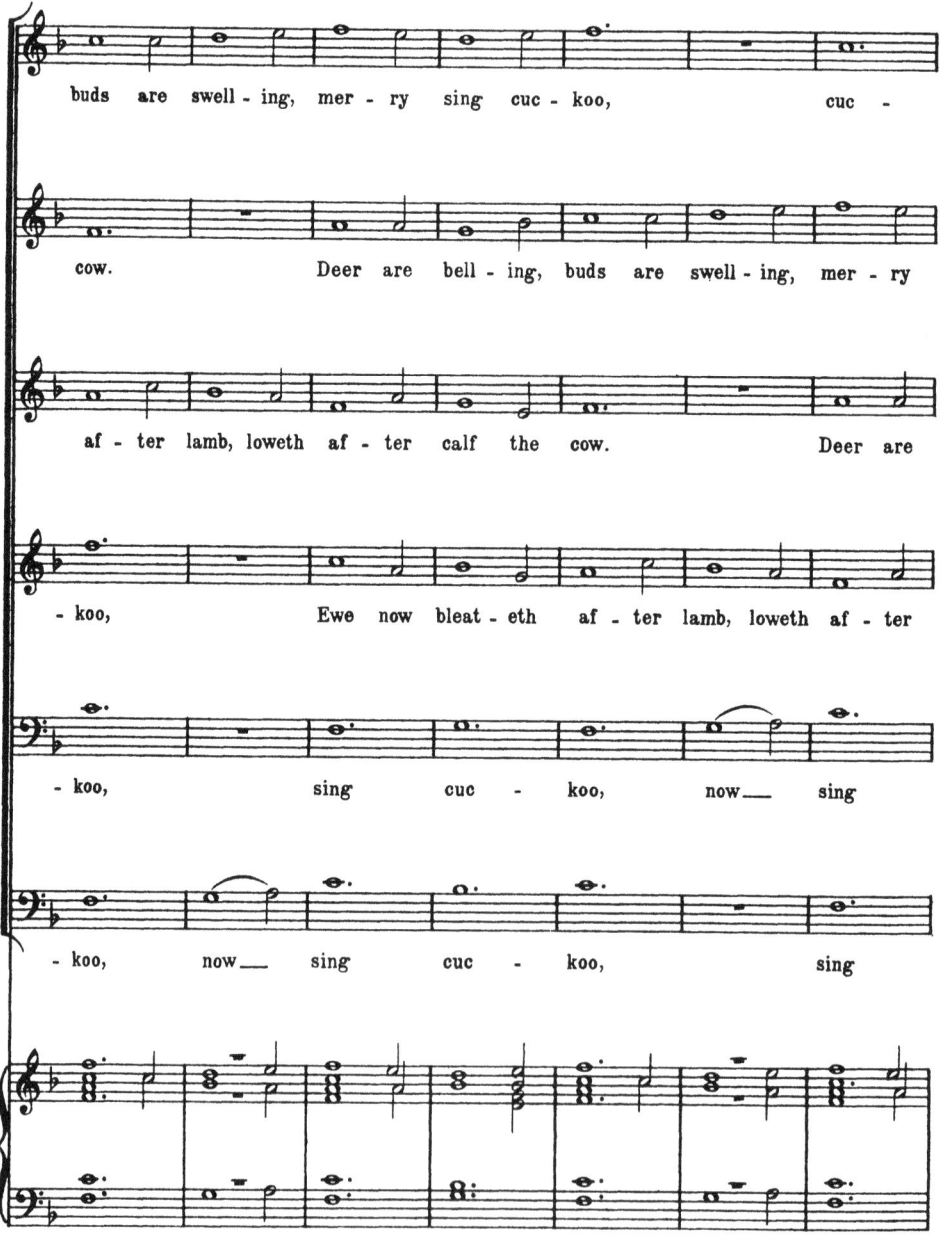

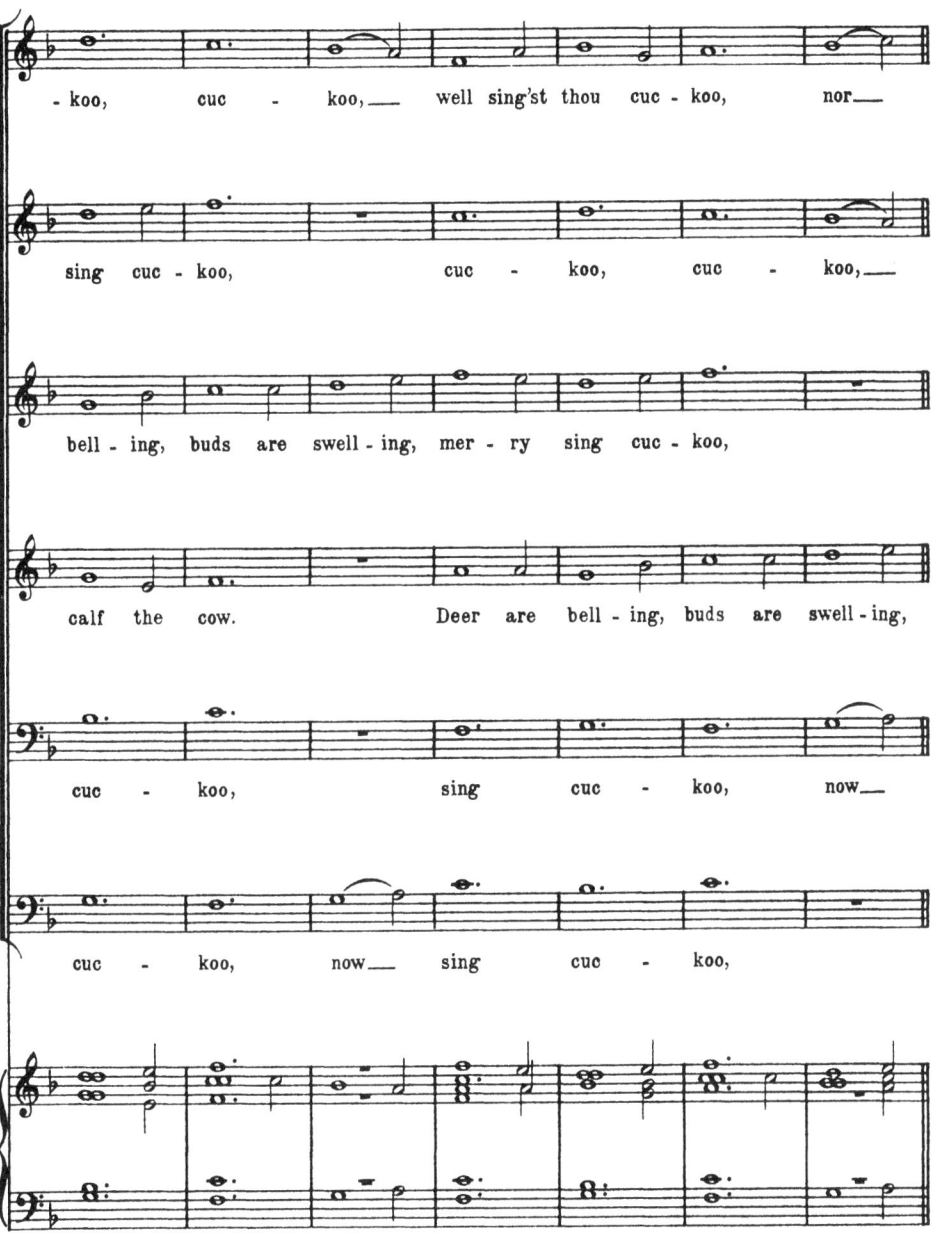

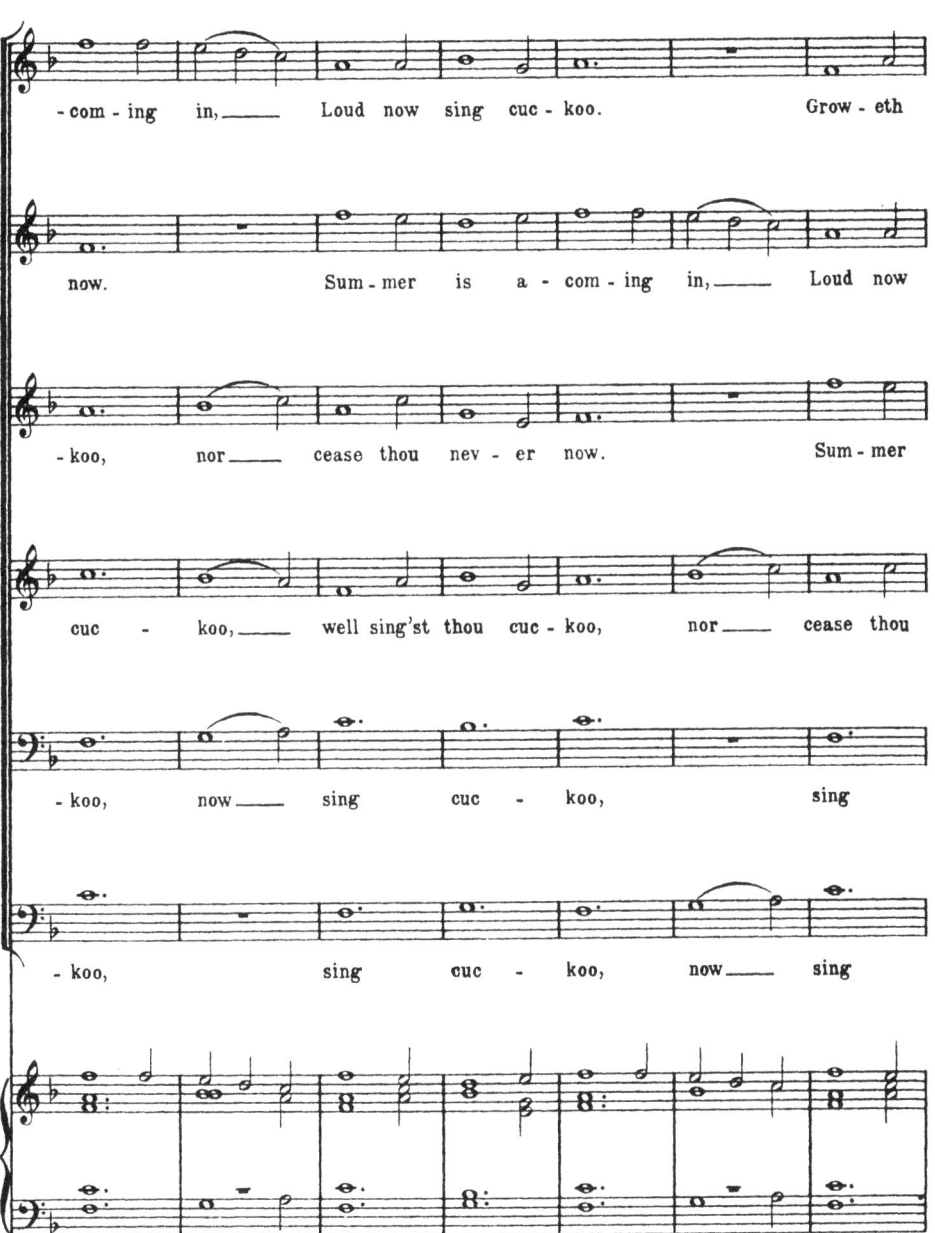

For EU product safety concerns, contact us at Calle de José Abascal, 56–1°,
28003 Madrid, Spain or eugpsr@cambridge.org.

www.ingramcontent.com/pod-product-compliance
Ingram Content Group UK Ltd.
Pitfield, Milton Keynes, MK11 3LW, UK
UKHW051009240426
470322UK00018B/577